# carving

## HOW TO CARVE WOOD AND STONE

### by Harvey Weiss

**▲ ADDISON-WESLEY**

## THE BEGINNING ARTIST'S LIBRARY

OTHER TITLES BY THE SAME AUTHOR IN THE

## BEGINNING ARTIST'S LIBRARY

1. CLAY, WOOD & WIRE
   *an introduction to sculpture*

2. PAPER, INK & ROLLER
   *beginning printmaking*

3. PENCIL, PEN & BRUSH
   *drawing in many media*

4. STICKS, SPOOLS & FEATHERS
   *varied craft projects*

5. CERAMICS—FROM CLAY TO KILN
   *an introduction to ceramics*

6. PAINT, BRUSH AND PALETTE
   *beginning painting*

7. COLLAGE AND CONSTRUCTION
   *an introduction*

8. LENS AND SHUTTER
   *an introduction to photography*

9. HOW TO MAKE YOUR OWN MOVIES
   *an introduction to filmmaking*

 **A Young Scott Book**

Text Copyright © 1976 by Harvey Weiss. Illustrations Copyright © 1976 by Harvey Weiss. All Rights Reserved. Addison-Wesley Publishing Company, Inc., Reading, Massachusetts 01867. Printed in the United States of America. First Printing.

BCDEFGHIJK-WZ-7987

**Library of Congress Cataloging in Publication Data**

Weiss, Harvey.
  Carving: an introduction to wood and stone carving.

  "A Young Scott book."
  SUMMARY: Introduces the tools and techniques for carving wood and stone.
  1. Wood-carving—Juvenile literature. 2. Stone cutting—Juvenile literature. 3. Sculpture—Juvenile literature. [1. Wood carving. 2. Stone carving. 3. Sculpture.] I. Title.
TT199.7.W43        731.4'6        75-2337
ISBN 0-201-09160-7

# CONTENTS

Thanks and acknowledgements are due to the following individuals and organizations who generously assisted the author: The American Museum of Natural History, The Museum of Modern Art, The Brooklyn Museum, The Field Museum of Natural History, The Newark Museum, The Mariners' Museum, The Metropolitan Museum of Art, The Solomon R. Guggenheim Museum, The Peabody Museum, The New York State Historical Society, Mr. Irving Sabo, Mr. Henry Moore, and especially Mr. Chaim Gross who very graciously permitted the author to make use of many of his photographs including the series on pages 40 and 41.
All drawings and sculpture not otherwise credited are by the author.

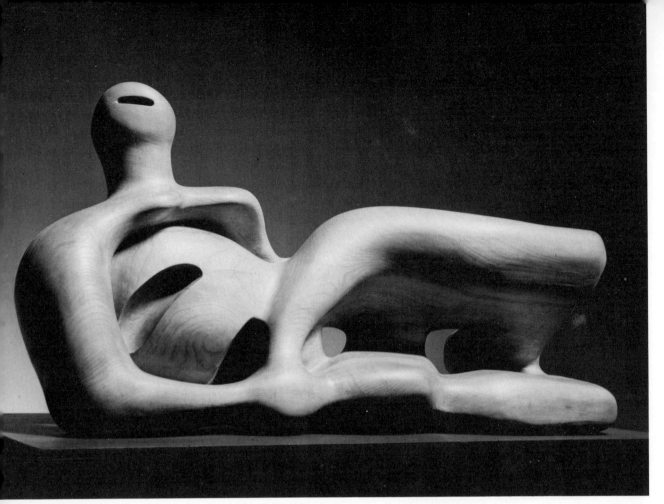

RECLINING FIGURE, Henry Moore, Elmwood

# Introduction

Carving is different from other kinds of sculpture. When you work with clay, wax, paper-mache, or materals of this sort the sculpture is built up. You start with nothing and gradually construct the shapes and forms you want. You add, shift about, take off, constantly change until you get a result you are satisfied with.

You can't do this when you are carving. With carving you start with a solid block of wood or stone and chip away, gradually removing material. Once a chip is removed it can't be replaced.

This sometimes seems a little alarming to many people. It seems so final—no chance to correct mistakes. But actually, you'll find that once you are started and have the feeling of your tools and the wood and stone you are working on you will have good control over what is happening. If you do make a mistake (everybody does) and cut off too much it is easy enough to alter your design somewhat to make allowances for the mistake. Sometimes a mistake is actually an improvement. Art is full of accidents.

Once you start to carve you will find that wood and stone have a very definite personality all their own. The wood or stone will have ''ideas of its own.'' There are shapes and forms that the material will forbid you to make! Let's take an example. Suppose you had a block of wood and decided to carve out of it a head with a nose like the one illustrated in the margin. You couldn't. It would be almost impossible because the grain of the wood runs up and down. A thin shape with the grain running across it is very weak. A slight bump or the least bit of pressure on this nose would snap it right off.

If you were determined to make a head with a pointy nose you could look for a log that had a branch protruding. The grain runs the long way through the branch, so you could use this for the nose. Another way to handle the situation would be

CHILD WITH CAT, William Zorach, Marble, Collection of The Museum of Modern Art, New York

5

to get a separate piece of wood with the grain running the right way, then glue it on, or set it into a hole drilled in the head.

If you were carving a piece of stone and wanted this same problem nose you would be out of luck. Stone is simply not strong when it is carved into thin or delicate shapes. It is only strong when it remains in bulky, compact form.

Very often you will find a material which already has a rough shape of some sort. You might, for example, find a piece of tree trunk which separates into two branches, a piece of driftwood with a peculiar shape, a piece of stone with odd proportions. And in these cases you will have to fit your idea to the material. Or, to say it in a different way, let the material suggest to you the kind of design that will work best. The wood or stone can tell you what should be carved.

There is something else about carving that makes it different from modelling in a soft material. And that is the beauty of the wood or stone you use. There is a great variety of color and pattern, and it is very satisfying to roll up your sleeves and work on these materials.

A large part of this book is devoted to various specific projects—how to carve a head, animals, and so on. Where there are technical matters the directions are quite exact. But the instructions are much more general when it comes to matters of taste and judgement. After all, when you decide to carve something you want to make what you want, not what I want. The final carving is going to be your proud possession—not mine. And besides, the materials you have to work with may be quite different from what is suggested in the text. Even if you did want to follow exact instructions you might not be able to.

There are a great many illustrations of carvings throughout this book, so if you are looking for ideas refer to these and then combine, change, eliminate, add your own ideas. In this way you will end up with something which is all your own and which you can be truly proud of.

# Part One
# CARVING WOOD

# 1. Materials and Tools

## Wood

There is an enormous variety of woods. There are strange and exotic woods like cocabola and satinwood and African zebrawood. And there are the more common woods like pine and oak and walnut and cedar. All these woods vary greatly in hardness and in color. And they all have a definite grain structure.

The grain of wood is produced by the normal growing action of the tree. It runs up and down the trunk and along the branches. The cellular structure of the tree produces this grain, and it is the means by which the tree gets its nourishment from the soil. Grain is very much the concern of anyone who is going to have anything to do with wood. It is important because: 1. It affects the way you use your cutting tools. 2. It has a lot to do with the strength of the forms you cut out.

A chisel works best when it is used to cut *with* the grain, or *across* the grain. If you try to cut against the grain you will split the wood or get large, unpredictable, jagged splinters. A chisel is intended to cut small, neat *chips* of wood. Easy does it—a little bit at a time! Don't ever try to gouge out big, splintery chunks of wood.

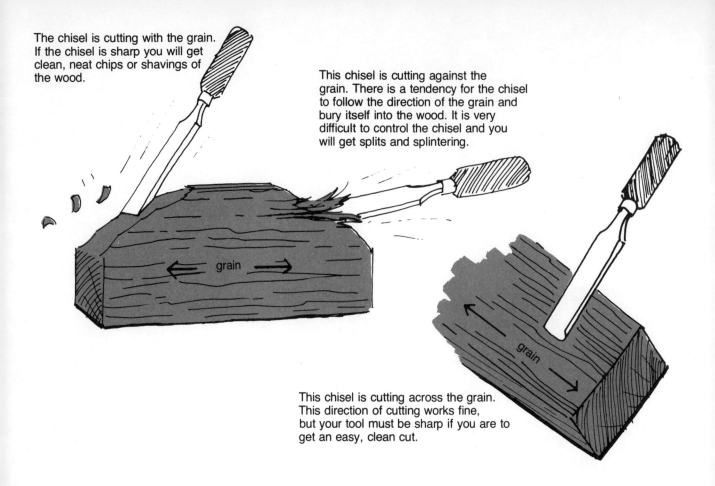

The chisel is cutting with the grain. If the chisel is sharp you will get clean, neat chips or shavings of the wood.

This chisel is cutting against the grain. There is a tendency for the chisel to follow the direction of the grain and bury itself into the wood. It is very difficult to control the chisel and you will get splits and splintering.

grain

This chisel is cutting across the grain. This direction of cutting works fine, but your tool must be sharp if you are to get an easy, clean cut.

grain

The grain of the wood is also a consideration when you are carving thin or protruding shapes. As in the case of the pointy nose mentioned on page 5, the grain should always run along with the main direction of thin or delicate forms. Very often separate pieces of wood are joined together so that the grain of the wood will be going the right way.

## Where to Get Wood

Many of the projects discussed in this book use planks or boards of wood. It shouldn't be hard to find this sort of thing. If you know someone who has a home woodworking shop you should be able to find a few leftover boards that will suit you. In many homes there are some pieces of wood, perhaps leftover shelving, or discarded wood furniture that can be used. Don't be discouraged if the wood you find is painted or dirty looking. Chip away a corner to see what kind of wood is underneath. It is amazing the way a scruffy-looking piece of wood can turn out to be clean and dry and straight-grained once the outside surface is cut away.

The one kind of wood to stay away from is plywood. Because this wood is built up of several thin layers with the grain running in different directions it is very difficult to carve. You might be able to use it where flat surfaces with no carving are needed or if a flat panel is to be attached to another larger piece. But, in general, it is best avoided.

Although boards or planks will do for some carving projects, a log or thick block of wood is needed for others. This can be a little difficult to find. If you live in the country you will be able to find a suitable piece in a wood pile. Or you may know where a tree has been cut down and the trunk sawn into short lengths. Sometimes a lumberyard will have an odd block of some sort, forgotten and tucked away in a back corner. In any event, all lumberyards carry what are called "four by fours." This is a kind of lumber used in house construction. It is usually fir or pine and measures a little less than 4 inches by 4 inches and can be had in just about any length you want. Most lumberyards however will be reluctant to cut off a short one or two foot length so you may end up buying wood enough for several carvings—or one very long totem pole!

Another way to get a block of wood is to build it up by carefully glueing several boards together. If the boards fit together snugly with no warps or gaps this is just as good as a single solid block of wood. More about how this is done on page 11.

## What Kind of Wood to Use

It might seem that a very soft wood is easiest for someone about to carve for the first time. This is not so. The softer a wood is, the sharper the tools must be. And very often the softness of the wood prevents the crisp forms and clean chisel marks which are so important in wood carving. A soft wood like balsa is all right for whittling model airplanes, but it is not much good for carving. On the other hand, an extremely tough wood like ebony or maple is simply too hard to work unless you are a very experienced carver.

Cost is another factor. Some woods are quite expensive. A thick, wide plank of good mahogany—assuming you could find it in a lumberyard—might be five or six dollars. Walnut would probably cost even more.

The most easily obtained wood, and the wood used by most beginners is plain old pine. If you are going to get your wood from a lumberyard this is the one kind you can be sure they will have in stock. Pine comes in different grades. Number two grade is used for many carpentry projects but it isn't too good for carving because it will have knotholes. A few small knotholes aren't too bad, but when there are big, rough, dark areas in the wood they will cause you all kinds of problems. Clear pine is another grade of pine. It is without knotholes and is ideal for most of the carving described in this book. Unfortunately most clear pine comes only in boards no more than one-inch thick. This is fine for some projects, but if you need a thick block of wood you will have to either glue together several boards or look for some other kind of wood which comes in heavier sizes.

Other woods that can be used for carving and which are found most everywhere are fir and redwood. Redwood has a conspicuous grain pattern, a deep color, and is often available in two-inch thick planks or four by four inch columns. However, it is a little too soft and "mushy" to carve well. Some other woods that are often used for carving are oak, cedar, mahogany, walnut, chestnut, elm, apple.

When you choose wood to carve avoid any that is checked. "Checked" is the term used by people who work with wood to describe splits and cracks. Most planks or logs will have a few small checks at the ends. This is sometimes impossible to avoid. But very large checks will cause you all kinds of troubles and any wood that has them should be passed by.

Another thing to watch out for is wood that has a lot of resin in it. You may come across logs which seem to be oozing a very sticky, glue-like gook. Certain kinds of pine trees are like this. This resin will get on your tools and all over you and make things generally disagreeable. It is also best not to use wood that has been lying about in damp places absorbing water. Wet wood is hard to carve. Serious wood carvers will find logs of a kind they like and let them sit around under cover for years drying out thoroughly before starting to work on them.

## Laminating

"Laminating" means glueing two or more boards together in order to get a more bulky piece of wood to carve. It is most important that the boards you are going to laminate are flat and come into complete contact with one another. If there are spaces between the layers you may cut into them as you work, and there will be unsightly gaps and jagged splinters.

This is how it is done: 1. Cut the boards you are going to glue together to the same size. 2. Make sure there is no grease or paint on the surfaces that will be glued. Don't use boards that are bent or warped. 3. Mix your glue and apply it liberally to the surfaces that will come in contact with one another. Use a good, strong carpenter's glue, or a white glue such as Elmer's. (You will need quite a bit of it.) 4. Finally, clamp the boards together. "C" clamps will work well if you have several good-sized ones. You can also wrap rope around the boards and then tighten up by means of wedges or twisting the rope. If the boards are flat and true and fit together well you may not need as much pressure, and can simply pile up a lot of weight on top of the boards. 5. Allow the glue to dry for as long as the directions on the container say. Then remove the clamps, rope, or weights, as the case may be, and you have a block of wood that is as strong, if not stronger, than a piece cut from a single log.

## LAMINATING WOOD

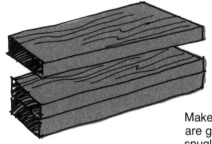

Don't skimp on the glue.

Here are some of the ways to keep the wood under pressure:

Make sure the boards you are glueing together fit snugly with no spaces.

Wrap with rope and wedge tight.

Pile up a lot of really heavy weights.

Use "C" clamps.

Put it in a vise.

The label on the glue container will tell you how long to keep the wood under pressure.

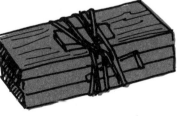

### The Tools

Almost any kind of chisel or gouge can be used to carve with—on one condition. And that is that the edge be razor sharp! A dull chisel will bruise your wood rather than cut it. It is very annoying and frustrating to try to work with dull tools. Don't attempt to carve wood until your chisels are as sharp as you can possibly make them. For this reason one of the most important tools listed below is the sharpening stone. Read the paragraphs about how to sharpen your tools with special care. Then take plenty of time to get your tools as sharp as you can.

### The Sharpening Stone

This is a rectangular stone with a coarse grit on one side and a fine grit on the other. A few drops of oil are put on the stone and then the bevel of the tool is rubbed back and forth. (You always sharpen the bevel on the tool, not the flat side.) It is very important that the tool be held firmly and steadily at a constant angle so that the bevel remains true. You don't want to round it off. The tool is rubbed on the coarse side of the stone first. Then the stone is turned over and the sharpening completed on the fine side. Finish off by laying your chisel bevel side up on the stone, and rub off the little burr which the sharpening process produces on the very edge of the blade.

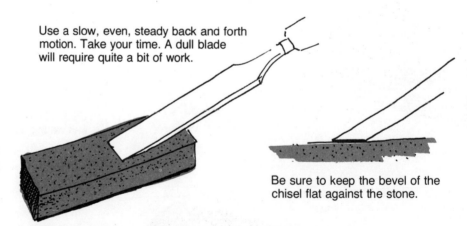

Use a slow, even, steady back and forth motion. Take your time. A dull blade will require quite a bit of work.

Keep the stone oiled so that the metal that comes off the chisel won't clog the stone.

Be sure to keep the bevel of the chisel flat against the stone.

Test the blade by trying it on a scrap of wood or by shaving off a bit of hair from your forearm. If you don't get an easy shave go back to work and sharpen some more!

The sharpening of a gouge (a "U" shaped chisel) is more

difficult than sharpening a straightedge chisel. In this case the gouge must be *rotated* as it is pushed back and forth on the sharpening stone. It may seem awkward at first. But with a little practice you'll be able to get an even, steady motion.

If you are using some old chisels and gouges which have been banging around in an old tool box, or if they have been used as screwdrivers or to open paint cans, they will be nicked and very dull. You will have a big job getting them back into usable condition. A grindstone, if you can get the use of one, will greatly speed up the sharpening process. If you use one be sure to: 1. Wear goggles to protect your eyes. 2. Keep dipping the chisel into water so that it won't overheat and lose its temper. 3. Go slowly and carefully making sure you keep the bevel straight and true. After the tool has been roughly sharpened on the grindstone you still have to use a sharpening stone for the final sharpening.

using a grindstone

**Chisels**    The term "chisel" is used to describe straight-edge chisels as well as gouges. Gouges are "U" shaped and are actually much more useful in carving than the straightedge chisels. Like any tools, chisels will vary greatly in quality. If you are going to use the chisels that you may find around your house you don't have much choice. But if you are going to buy chisels get the best you can afford. The cheap tools that are found in cut-rate variety stores are made with poor steel and won't hold an edge.

There are special chisels made for wood carving. These can be found at a well-equipped art store or a good hardware store. They are available in sets, complete with sharpening stone and mallet. But they are very expensive. There is one wood carver's chisel with which you can do most anything. It is a gouge like the one illustrated in the margin. If you are going out to buy wood carving tools and have only a limited amount of money to spend, you would be much better off getting one top-quality gouge which is made for carving rather than a few cheap gouges and chisels which are meant for carpentry work.

The plain carpenter's chisels are less expensive than the wood carver's chisels. They are more rugged, but won't do as good a job even if they are kept razor sharp. A good selection of chisels for a start would be a one-inch straightedge chisel, and a 5/8th-inch gouge.

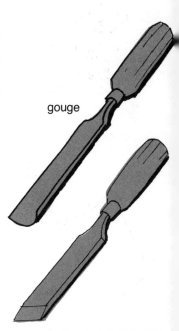

gouge

straightedge chisel

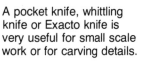

A pocket knife, whittling knife or Exacto knife is very useful for small scale work or for carving details.

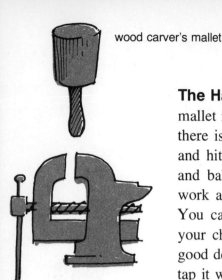

wood carver's mallet

a machinist's vise

a woodworker's vise

## The Hammer

Professional wood carvers use a wooden mallet instead of a hammer. The mallet has a larger surface so there is less chance of swinging at the chisel handle, missing, and hitting one of your fingers. It also has a different weight and balance so that a short, tapping stroke will do as much work as a long swing with a hammer. But it is not essential. You can get by with the ordinary claw hammer. Actually, if your chisels are sharp, you won't need a hammer at all for a good deal of the finish cutting. You can just push the chisel, or tap it with the heel of your hand and get a neat, clean chip.

## The Vise

Unless you are working on a very large and heavy piece of wood such as a big log, you will need some means of holding your work as you carve it. A good-sized vise is the most useful kind of holder. What you need is a heavy woodworker's vise or a large machinist's vise. The small vise that clamps to a tabletop isn't much good because the constant hammering will soon make it come loose.

There are other ways of holding a piece of wood while you work on it. Very often it is possible to nail a block of wood onto your worktable. Then you can place your work up against this block. This will keep it from slipping about. A large "C" clamp can also be used to hold the work.

## Other Tools

A saw is useful for quickly removing odd corners or big chunks of wood. It is also necessary when several pieces of board have to be cut up and glued together. Another kind of very useful saw has a thin removable blade. It is called a coping saw and comes in handy for cutting curves and small shapes. A wood rasp and a file or two will also come in handy when you want to get a very smooth or polished surface. A sharp wood rasp will actually cut away wood in record time. There is another tool, similiar to a rasp, which is called a hand shaper. It has a perforated, replaceable blade and will do the work of a rasp, but neater and with less effort. A drill with varied size bits will also prove useful at times.

coping saw

rasp

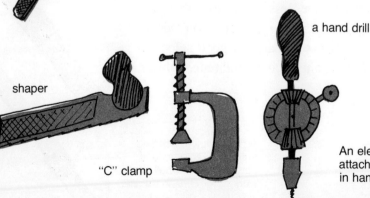

shaper

"C" clamp

a hand drill

If you are working on a large piece of wood with hammer and chisel and the chips are flying, it is essential that you wear a pair of safety goggles to protect your eyes!

An electric drill with a sanding attachment will very often come in handy.

# EXPERIMENTING WITH YOUR TOOLS

Unless you've done a lot of wood carving, it is a very good idea to get a few pieces of wood and spend a little time experimenting to see what can or cannot be done with the tools you have to work with. An hour or so trying out your tools in all kinds of different ways will teach you a great deal.

Before you work on any wood try to figure out the direction in which the grain goes.

Are your tools razor sharp?

Try cutting with the grain and see what happens.

Try cutting against the grain and see what the results are. (You'll get splits.)

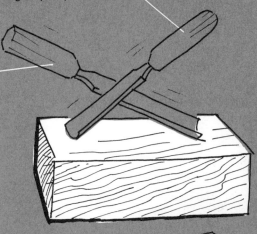

*Important* →

Remember to always keep your hand away from the front of the blade. Assume that the tool is going to slip! When it does will your hand be in its path?

Cut across the grain of the wood.

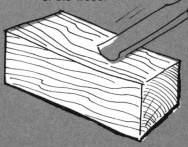

See if you can cut across the end of a piece of wood. You'll find that this is quite hard to do.

A lot of detailed and small scale carving can be done with a sharp pocketknife.

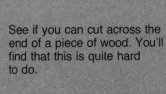

A vertical cut down into wood is called a "stop cut." It will keep the wood from splintering when later you cut towards it from a different direction.

A good way to get familiar with your cutting tools is by carving different patterns into a board. See if you can cut a three-cornered chip with just three strokes of your straight-edge chisel.

Be sure your wood is held securely. You can't carve wood that is sliding about or held with one hand. The wood should be in a vise or somehow clamped to your work table. If you don't have a vise or clamps nail a block of wood to the table and place your work against it.

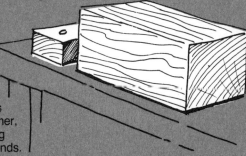

Try using your chisels with a mallet or hammer, and try simply pushing the tools with your hands.

The shark has been carved out of a four by four inch piece of cedar. The fin was made separately and glued on. The grain of the wood is so nice the wood was left unpainted. (If you turn the shark upside down, it looks like a whale.)

This polka-dotted fish was made from a piece of one-inch pine board.

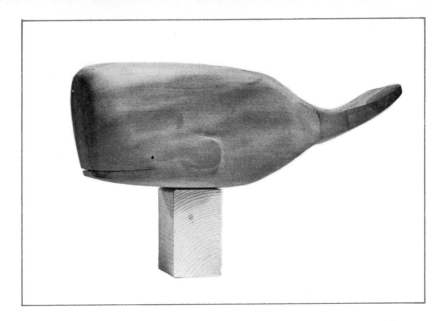

# 2. Getting Started— Carving a Fish

This is a simple kind of carving that can't help but turn out well. The shapes are quite easy to carve. If you have never done any carving before this is a good project to start with. It will let you get familiar with your tools and you won't run into any tricky or complicated problems.

**Materials**  A plank of wood is needed for the body. A convenient size would be 1″ thick, 6″ wide and 12″ long. But this is a matter that is up to you. If you use a board that is only one-inch thick you are going to end up with a rather thin fish. If you want a fatter one use a thicker board or glue together two or more boards. You may also want a small block of wood for the base and a round stick (called a dowel) to support your fish.

**1.**  Draw the outline of your fish on the board. Don't worry about getting a realistic drawing with all the details. Just get a pleasant, streamlined shape.

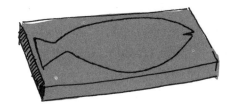

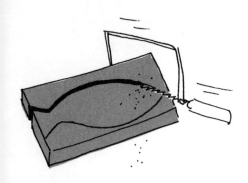

**2.** Now cut away the wood up to your outline. If your fish is small you could do this by simply whittling with a sharp pocket knife. Another way you could do it is with a coping saw. You could also put the wood in a vise and cut out the shape with hammer and chisel. If you do it this way pay attention to the grain and remember to cut with or across the grain, not against it.

**3.** Next round off the sharp edges. Give your fish a rounded, smooth shape that is nice to touch. Your gouge or a rasp will do a quick job of this.

**4.** Cut or file a notch under the head to indicate the gills. You can make the eye by drilling or using a nail to punch a hole. Smooth with a rasp or file. Sandpaper for a really smooth surface.

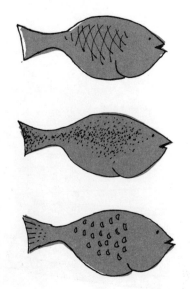

**5.** Now you must consider the matter of the fish's skin, or scales. You may decide not to bother with this at all, or else paint on a pattern of scales when you are finished. If you want you can suggest the scales by giving the wood a texture of some sort. You can be realistic and make rows of shallow arcs using your gouge. Or you can be fanciful and try various combinations of dents, holes, gouges, or scratches. If you are using a wood like redwood which has a fairly strong grain, you probably wouldn't want to bother with any additional surface texture. If you are going to carve a texture on your fish, experiment with a scrap of wood before you start banging away on the fish itself.

**6.** You can mount the fish by simply filing a flat spot at the bottom and glueing it on a block of wood. Or you might prefer the dowel arrangement which will make the fish look like it is floating. Drill a hole in the base and in the fish and then glue a dowel in place as shown.

**7.** If you have a nice piece of wood and you like the color and pattern of the grain, you can simply sandpaper all over, rub on a little wax and consider the job finished. But if you prefer you can paint it. If your fish is a tropical fish you have an excuse for some bright, wild colors.

The fins are best made separately. Whittle the base into the form of a peg, then glue it into an appropriately sized hole.

The tail can be made separately and then glued into a slot.

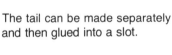

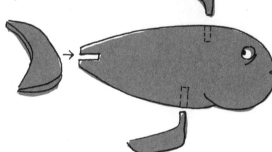

Some fish look very nice hung from the ceiling. In this case you need a screw eye at the center of balance. (You can make several small fish and arrange them into a mobile.)

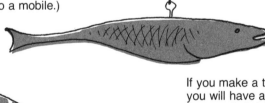

If you make a tropical fish you will have an excuse to do a really bright, colorful paint job.

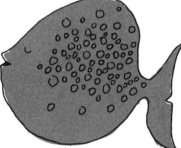

Eagle of painted wood, carved
in the early 1800's in Pennsylvania,
The Metropolitan Museum of Art

The way to make this little
bird is explained on the
next few pages.

This "bird" is a simple, flat
silhouette cut out of a thin
board. He'd look nice on the
peak of a barn or on a pole
out of doors. From the collection
of the New York State Historical
Association, by an unknown
artist.

20

# 3. Carving a Bird

Birds are quite simple to make, even though they may seem rather difficult at first glance. The open wings on the body look as though they would be hard to carve. And they would be if these birds were cut out of a single block of wood. But the wings are made separately out of thin wood and attached after the body has been shaped. A flock of birds like these, hanging from the ceiling of any room and moving about in the slightest breeze, is great fun.

**Materials**      A piece of 2″ by 2″ pine 6″ long will do for the body. You could, of course, glue together two or more boards to get the size you wanted. For the wings you need two pieces of thin wood about 3″ wide and 5″ long. See if you can get some flat stripping or molding about ⅜″ thick. Plywood is best avoided, but if you can't find anything else you may have to settle for this. If you want your bird to stand rather than fly from the ceiling you'll need two lengths of ¼″ dowel and a block of wood for a base.

**1.**      Make the body first. You can carve it with hammer and chisel, or you can "carve" it with a coping saw, as shown in the photographs on page 24. Keep the forms simple, flowing and graceful! (If you have the bird in a metal vise and are using a chisel, be careful not to let it slip and strike the metal. This will badly nick the blade.) This bird could also be whittled into shape if you have a sharp pocketknife and you are using an easy-to-cut wood such as pine.

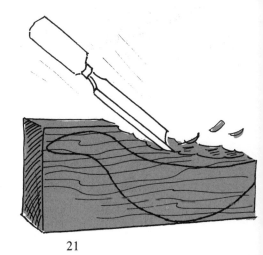

21

**2.** If your cutting tools leave a nice, crisp surface on the wood, you may decide to leave this texture as the final surface and do no more finishing. Or you can use a rasp, file, and sandpaper to get a really smooth surface if that is your preference.

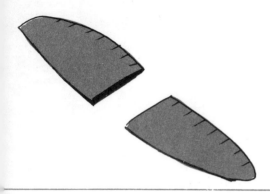

**3.** Make the wings next. File off all the sharp edges and corners. Try to get a sleek, streamlined shape. Experiment with a scrap piece of wood to see if you can suggest the feathers in some way. Try cutting shallow grooves or notches. If you don't like the way this looks simply leave the wings smooth. The back edges of the wings can be cut or filed into a jagged or scalloped edge.

**4.** Now cut a notch in the back of the bird into which the wings will fit. Do this carefully and neatly so that you get a tight fit. Notice that the notch is shaped in such a way that the wings are angled upwards. If you want the wings to go straight out you can make the notch straight across the back of the bird. This is something for you to decide for yourself.

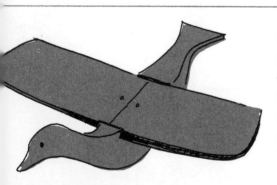

**5.** Glue the wings in place. If you don't trust the glue to hold the wings securely use a nail or screw for extra strength. If you do nail or screw, drill a hole in the wings first. This will keep the wood from splitting. (A nail or screw used near the edge of a board is always likely to cause the wood to split unless a "pilot" hole is first drilled.)

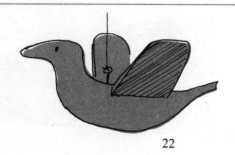

**6.** If your bird is to "fly" add a small screw eye in the back where you judge the center of weight to be. A thread can be tied to the screw eye and your bird hung from the ceiling.

**7.** If you want your bird to stand, drill two holes in its belly into which two dowel legs can be glued. Then cut out a piece of wood for a base and drill another two holes for the lower ends of the dowels.

**8.** There are a number of different ways of finishing your bird. You can leave the wood untouched, waxed, stained, or painted. If you have made a few accidental gouges or if there is some splintering you couldn't carve away, you may have to use some plastic wood for a little patching. In this case you don't have much choice except to paint, because you will want to hide the patching. (You can make your own plastic wood by mixing fine filings or sawdust with glue.)

Here are a few suggestions for some other kinds of birds you might want to make.

tail feathers made separately

# MAKING A BIRD

1. The profile is drawn on the wood. This is a piece of 4″ by 4″ cedar.

2. The profile has been cut out with a coping saw, and the top outline is drawn.

3. Now the top outline has been sawed away.

4. The bird is held in a vise and a gouge is being used.

5. A shaper being used to round off the body.

6. Holes for the legs are being drilled.

7. The body has been sanded smooth and the dowels set in place.

8. The finished bird with wings set into notches cut in the back.

# HOW TO MAKE A DECOY

The decoy described here is made in the same way a large model boat is made—that is, the "bread and butter" method. It is given this name because several layers of wood with the center area cut out are "buttered" with glue and then stuck together. This makes for a buoyant, lightweight, but very strong type of construction. Commercial decoys are often constructed of cork, plastic, and various other materials, but our hand carved duck will be in the traditional, old-fashioned style.

Decoys are quite easy and fun to make even if you never intend to shoot a duck. And a decoy makes a very handsome decoration.

1. Cut four 1″ thick, 6″ wide boards to the same length.

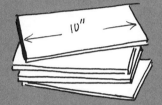

2. Cut all four boards to an oval or tear-drop shape. Use a coping saw for this.

3. Cut out the center of the two middleboards. To do this you must first drill a hole. Then remove the blade from the coping saw. Pass it through the hole, reattach it and saw away.

4. Glue all four boards together. Use a waterproof glue if your decoy is to go to sea.

5. With a chisel, shaper, or rasp round off the body on top and bottom. A decoy looks a little like a squashed-down football. File a long groove in the back.

6. Cut out the head from a 2″ thick piece of wood, or two 1″ pieces that have been glued together. Shape it carefully.

7. Glue on the head. Patch any gaps with plastic wood. Sandpaper carefully.

The decoy should be shaped and painted to resemble a particular kind of duck. The one shown here is a male canvasback.

If you are going to use the decoy in the water, attach a little keel. Then fasten a weight to the bottom of the keel. This will make it float in a more realistic way.

RENEE, Chaim Gross, Sabacu wood,
Collection of the Tel Aviv Museum, Israel

Wood carving from British Columbia,
American Museum of Natural History

African wood carving,
American Museum of Natural History

# 4. Carving a Head

As you can see from the illustrations there are many ways to carve a head. The head by Chaim Gross is a portrait of the sculptor's wife. Even though this is a fairly realistic carving, the shapes are simplified and we get the feeling that the artist was as much interested in showing the beauty of the wood as he was in getting an accurate portrait. The tool marks on this head show very clearly and make an interesting texture. Only the lips and eyes have been polished.

The other heads are quite fanciful and there hasn't been much of an effort to get a realistic likeness. The head on the right has been painted, and small shells have been set into the mouth to indicate teeth.

**Materials**     If you can find a log you will have an excellent material for carving a head. It doesn't have to be very large. Six or eight inches in diameter is a good size, and about twelve inches in length is about right for most heads. The wood should be dry and without big cracks or splits. Before you choose a log to work on, it is a good idea to carve away a corner to remove the bark and see what the wood is really like. If it turns out to be too hard, or rotted, or too wet, or too full of resin, discard it and look for something else.

If you can't find a log—and a log is something that isn't too easy to come by if you live in a big city or suburban community—you will have to "build" a block of wood for yourself. This is simply a matter of glueing together three or four pieces of board. Read the paragraphs on laminating, page 11, for directions on how to do this.

Still another possibility is to look for a piece of 4″ by 4″ construction lumber.

**1.** Begin by taking the bark off the log, if that is what you have to work with. Then take a good long look at the log—or block of wood, as the case may be. See if there are any knotholes, or special turns and twists in the wood that suggest anything to you. You might find a flaw at just where you expect the tip of the nose will be. In a case like this you would want to turn the wood around, or change your ideas (or nose) to suit the wood. Decide which end of the wood will be the top, which the front. Make sure the bottom of the wood is flat so that it stands up straight without wobbling.

**2.** With a piece of charcoal, crayon, or soft pencil draw the location of the key points—chin, nose, eyes, ears. This will serve as a kind of map or guide as you work.

**3.** Now you can begin to carve. (But don't be impatient and start unless your tools are as sharp as you can possibly get them! See page 13 about how to sharpen your tools.) You'll probably find that the gouge will be the tool you use more than any other. With a gouge you can "scoop" out a neat, clean chip with perfect control. Be aware of the grain of the wood and cut in such a direction that you avoid snags and splintering.

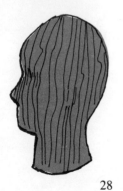

**4.** At the beginning you'll find that it is best to work for a while on the front of the head, then the back, then one side and then the other. This way you will have a feeling of how the entire head is shaping up. Don't bother with small details yet. Concentrate on getting the main, basic forms!

**5.** Don't be concerned with getting a realistic looking head. This is quite difficult in any kind of carving. Clay or plasticene would be a better material if you were trying to get an exact likeness of someone. Notice the way the pattern of the grain changes as you carve into the wood. If you find this particularly interesting see if you can't make the most of it. Alter your forms in order to accentuate these lines. As you work you may get different ideas about what you want to do. By all means make any changes that you feel like. There really isn't any reason why the head you started to carve shouldn't end up as a seated horse, or a whale, or a gorilla—as long as you are pleased with the results.

**6.** When you have all the main shapes blocked out you can begin to work on some of the smaller forms like mouth, ears, eyes. Keep these things simple. In many cases something as simple as a small hole will do for the eye. Sometimes a short line is all you need for the mouth. When you are working on these small details and delicate shapes, a sharp pocketknife will come in handy.

**7.** At this point you may want to use a file, then sandpaper to get smooth polished forms. This will help to show up the grain of the wood. But you must use judgement and care if you use these tools because it is very easy to simply round off all the forms, removing all the tool marks and some of the crisp look of the carving. Many carvings are left fairly rough with all the tool marks showing and with only a little polishing in selected areas. If your tools were sharp and you have a nice surface texture produced by your tools, you may want to leave it just this way.

**8.** When you are all finished you should give the wood a good heavy coat of wax. This will protect the wood and also bring up its natural color. If you don't particularly like the looks of your finished wood, or had to do a lot of patching, you may decide to paint it. In this case don't use wax, but give the wood a coat of shellac or varnish first. This will act as a sealer and the paint will go on much better.

## THE SHAPE OF A HEAD

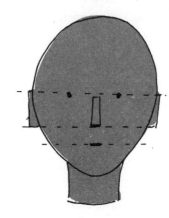
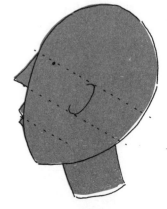

The average head is egg shaped.

The hair can be simplified into a few basic shapes and the texture of the tool marks can also be used to suggest it.

It is best to think of the head as being just a few, simple geometric shapes rather than a collection of small, realistic details.

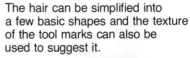

To make the nose stand out from the rest of the head the wood on both sides and below the tip must be carved away.

If you want a big nose or large ears, make them separately then glue them on.

Detail of statuette carved in the fifteenth century in England, The Metropolitan Museum of Art

30

This is a typical relief carving with nothing projecting above the surface of the wood board. The oval background has been stained a dark color and the head of the eagle was painted white.

Variation of the eagle shown on page 34.

# 5. Carving an Eagle in Relief

Any carving which is flattened out and attached to a background is called a relief carving. The sculpture on coins, for example, is relief sculpture. Sculpture which is rather flat, such as on coins, is called low relief. Sculpture which projects a good distance up from its background is called high relief.

The eagle is a traditional American symbol that is often found on old sailing ships and in colonial signs. It makes a handsome decoration when carefully carved out of a good solid plank of wood and is neatly painted. In many homes in New England an eagle is placed over the front door. It is also often used on the stern of boats, sometimes with a scroll on which the name of the boat is carved.

**Materials**　　All you need is a wide, thick board. Try to get a piece of pine. If that's not available you can get by with fir, spruce, cedar, mahogany, or most any wood that isn't too hard and that doesn't have a lot of knotholes. The wood should be dry and not full of sap. Stay away from wood that is badly warped or split. Get as wide and thick a piece of wood as possible. A plank 12" wide, 20" long, and 2" or more thick would be ideal. Large size scraps of plywood are often to be easily found, but don't be tempted to use them. They simply won't do, unless you are content to just cut out a flat silhouette shape of the eagle and then depend on your painting job to make it look good.

33

**1.** Draw the outline of the eagle on the wood. Allow room for about a half-inch of border.

**2.** Now start to cut away the background. The simplest way to do this is to make a vertical cut with your straightedge chisel along the edge of the eagle. Then chip away up to this cut. How much wood you chip away depends on the thickness of the board. If the board is only one-inch thick you can't very well remove more than a half-inch of wood.

**3.** The next step is to carve some of the shapes of the eagle itself. Round the chest. Shape the wings. Cut away the wood from around the claws so that they stand out clearly.

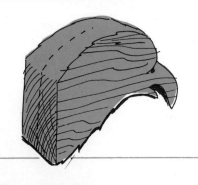

**4.** The head is made separately. Use two pieces of wood glued together, or one block of wood measuring about 2″ by 3″ by 3″. When it is finished glue it in place.

**5.** An important part of this carving is the feathers. This requires some thought and planning. Draw them on the wood carefully. Then try to be consistent as you carve them so that there is an even, over-all pattern.

34

**6.** The finished eagle will probably look best if carefully painted. The background can be brown or a soft green; the body and wings gold; the beak, neck, and talons white. These instructions can be changed as you see fit if you prefer an eagle more like one of the ones shown on the previous pages.

EAGLE, John Bellamy, Collection of the Mariners' Museum. This eagle is not in relief, but illustrates a way of handling the head and wings. This carving is actually a figurehead from an old sailing ship, the *Lancaster*. It is huge—about fifteen feet tall.

BALLERINA, Chaim Gross,
Collection of the Brooklyn Museum

KING OF KINGS, Constantin Brancusi,
The Solomon R. Guggenheim Museum

WOMAN AT THE PIANO, Elie Nadelman,
The Museum of Modern Art

HAWAIIAN WAR GOD,
The Peabody Museum

# 6. A Standing Figure

The standing figure is a subject that has always appealed to wood carvers. There is an enormous variety of styles and approaches, as you can see from the illustrations. But you may notice that most of the carvings have a basic, log-like shape. There are not many arms or legs sticking out. The forms are compact, condensed, squeezed together. This, of course, is because most of these figures were carved from a single log or block of wood which is a compact shape. There are very highly-skilled carvers who can cut delicate, free standing shapes, and are capable of carving the whiskers on a butterfly. But this is not very common and it is trying to do something with wood that wood really isn't intended for. In a way this kind of technical skill is fighting against the character of the wood.

It is, of course, possible to have thin shapes sticking out from a log or block of wood. This can be done either by finding a log with a branch sticking out, or else making a separate piece of wood and attaching it to the main piece.

When you have found a log or block of wood to work on look at it carefully and see if it doesn't suggest to you what to make. In carving this is often a better way of working rather than first getting an idea and then making your wood fit in with the idea.

**Materials**     A log will provide the material for most any kind of figure carving. If you can't get a log see if you can find a piece of 4″ by 4″ lumber. If you prefer to work larger, try and get a piece of 4″ by 6″, or 6″ by 6″ lumber. Lumber yards don't always stock lumber in short lengths, so if you go there you will have to try and get some odd or leftover pieces. And you

CAPTAIN JINKS,
The Newark Museum

37

may have to settle for whatever kind of wood there is . . . fir or redwood or pine or whatever. But don't take it if it is badly checked, wet or full of knotholes or sap. If all else fails you can get a plank of clear pine or something similiar, cut it up into suitable lengths, and glue it together to get a block that can be carved. See page 11 about laminating.

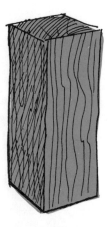

**1.**    The first thing you must do is very carefully look at the wood you have to work with. If you already have some ideas about what you want to carve, think about how your idea will fit into the size and shape of your wood. You may have to make some major changes in your original plan in order to get it to fit. If you have a piece of wood—and no ideas—then leaf through this book and see if some of the illustrations don't suggest something to you.

Let's assume that you had a piece of 4″ by 4″ wood and decided to make a medieval knight in armor. This is a fairly easy subject and makes a handsome little piece of sculpture. Before you do anything else make sure the base is level. If it isn't, chisel off the high spots or make a fresh cut with a saw.

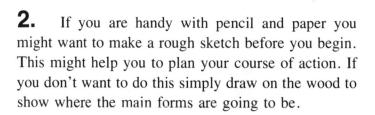

**2.**    If you are handy with pencil and paper you might want to make a rough sketch before you begin. This might help you to plan your course of action. If you don't want to do this simply draw on the wood to show where the main forms are going to be.

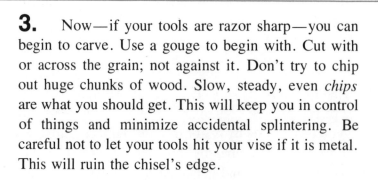

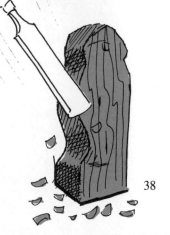

**3.**    Now—if your tools are razor sharp—you can begin to carve. Use a gouge to begin with. Cut with or across the grain; not against it. Don't try to chip out huge chunks of wood. Slow, steady, even *chips* are what you should get. This will keep you in control of things and minimize accidental splintering. Be careful not to let your tools hit your vise if it is metal. This will ruin the chisel's edge.

**4.** Work for a while on the front of the figure, then the back, then the sides. Try to think of your figure as being made up of a combination of simple geometric shapes; the head as a ball; the chest an egg shape; the legs as cylinders. If you think this way you will avoid the mushy, vague, indeterminate shapes that so many beginners get when they are indecisive and unsure.

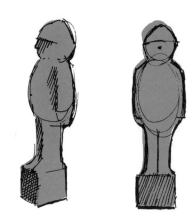

**5.** When the main forms are blocked out you can begin to work on some of the smaller forms. Try using a rasp or file in some areas and see if you like the results you get this way. Try using a sharp pocketknife for some of the hard-to-get-at corners. Use some of your own ideas about the kind of armor your knight is wearing. You may have some books with pictures of knights in armor that will give you some ideas. The fellow shown here is quite simplified and not very accurate historically.

**6.** Now you can apply the finishing touches. The edge of a file will engrave lines to indicate the joints in the armor. Or you can use a pocketknife to make a narrow "V" cut. You can punch shallow holes with a nail to indicate rivets, or you can actually hammer in short brass tacks. If you want your knight to hold a lance get a piece of stiff wire and put it through a hole drilled in his fist. A length of wire from a coat hanger will make a fine lance.

If you have a lot of accidental chips and splintering you may want to patch them up. Plastic wood will do the job. However, once you do any patching you will be forced to paint the wood. Otherwise you'll have a botchy look. If there aren't any patches and you like the way the wood looks, simply give it a rub with wax.

# CARVING A FIGURE

1. These photographs show how the well-known American sculptor, Chaim Gross carved a figure—actually, two figures—from a large log. To the right you can see a small clay model of the sculpture he was about to start.

2. A piece of chalk is used to show the main forms and shapes of the sculpture. The drawing is very simple and only serves as a rough guide.

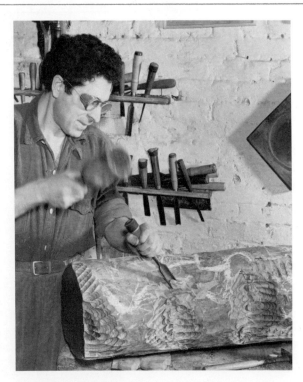

3. A large gouge is being used here for roughing out the main shapes. Notice that the sculptor is wearing a pair of safety goggles to protect his eyes from flying chips.

4. This log is heavy enough to stand up securely by itself as it is worked on. A smaller piece would have to be somehow clamped down or held in a vise.

5. The entire mass has been roughed out now, using a gouge. If you compare the sculpture as it stands now to the finished piece, you can see just what each shape is going to end up looking like.

6. As the work progresses a smaller gouge is used. This gives the sculptor more control and permits the carving of the smaller, more delicate shapes.

7 A rasp is being used here to remove the tool marks, because a smooth surface was wanted. Many sculptors like the texture left by the chisels and don't bother with this smoothing and polishing operation.

8 And here is the finished piece. It has been filed and polished as smooth as possible so that the color and grain show up. The work is called BALANCING and is now in the Philadelphia Museum of Fine Art.

This goat is fairly large, measuring 28 inches from nose to tail. It has been "built" from one long, pine board as explained in the text.

THE HORSE, Alexander Calder, The Museum of Modern Art. This horse is carved from walnut wood. The head and body are one piece and fit into notches cut in the front and rear legs.

# 7. An Animal Carving

A thin shape cut out of wood can be either strong or weak depending on the way the grain runs. Because of this you will find that there are some problems with certain kinds of carving. The horse shown below is an example of this. If you were carving it out of a piece of wood where the grain ran up and down, the legs would be strong but the neck and tail would be weak and likely to snap off. Suppose you turned the wood around so the grain ran horizontally, from front to back of the horse. Then the neck and tail would be strong, but the legs weak.

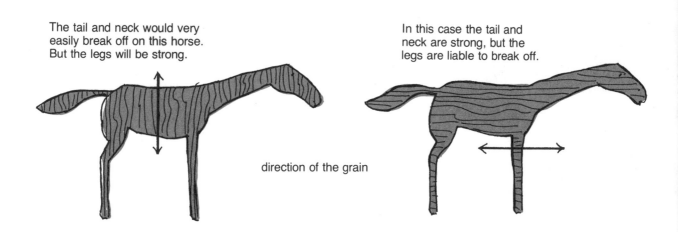

The tail and neck would very easily break off on this horse. But the legs will be strong.

In this case the tail and neck are strong, but the legs are liable to break off.

direction of the grain

The way to handle this is to use several different pieces of wood, each with the grain running in the direction that will give the most strength. In addition, this way of working is the only way if you want to work on a large scale. Large, solid blocks of wood are hard to find, and even the biggest log is not suitable for an animal two or three feet tall. The goat described here is built up from many smaller pieces of wood. It may seem like a pretty complicated undertaking. But it isn't. It is simpler than trying to carve it out of a single block of wood. It just seems complicated because there are so many pieces.

Although the following steps describe how this goat was put together you can use this same method, but change the proportions, to make all kinds of figures or animals. It would be easy enough to change the sizes and proportions given here and end up with a horse, a hippopotamus, a camel, a zebra, an ostrich, a dog, or whatever.

**Materials**  If you are going to make a goat like the one described here and want him to stand about 12″ high (that's a fairly big goat!) you will need eight feet of 1″ by 6″ board, and plenty of glue. An eight ounce bottle should be more than enough. A quick-drying, white glue, such as Elmer's, will work well.

IMPORTANT. Read complete directions (pages 44 through 49) before starting.

**1.**  Make a full size drawing of the animal you are going to build.

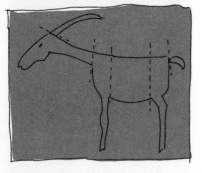

**2.**  Divide the drawing into its separate main parts—legs, body, neck and so on.

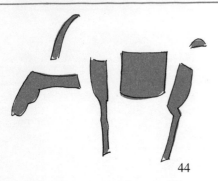

**3.**  Cut up the drawing so that there is a pattern for each part of the animal.

**4.** Trace these patterns onto your wood. You'll have two forelegs, two hind legs, three head and neck pieces (see step 9, page 46), and five body pieces (see step 9, page 46). Be careful that the grain of the wood is in a direction that will give the parts the most strength.

**5.** Make certain three of your five body pieces are a bit longer than your pattern because they are to fit between the hind legs (see step 9, page 46). Because the body is a more or less square shape, you don't have to worry about the direction of the grain. Cut out the five pieces.

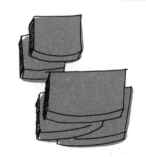

**6.** The legs are made next. They can be cut to the shape indicated with a coping saw. Don't attach anything yet. You can do that later after you've temporarily assembled all the parts and decide that they look the way you want.

**7.** Make certain the three neck and head pieces are a bit longer than your pattern because they are to fit between the forelegs (see step 9, page 46). Cut out the three pieces.

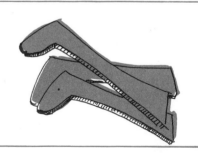

**8.** Glue together the three pieces that make up the head and neck. Carve it to shape before it is attached to the body. It is easier this way. Try to get the thin delicate-looking neck that is one of the nicest things about goats. A rasp or rough file will do the job fairly speedily.

**9.** Now fit everything temporarily together to see how it looks. If you're satisfied glue it all together, being sure to use weights or clamps for the recommended time.

It is important that the ends of all these pieces be cut and finished square and true so that they make good contact with one another. Otherwise the glue won't hold neck and body securely together.

These three pieces must be made longer than shown on the paper pattern because they must fit between the rear legs.

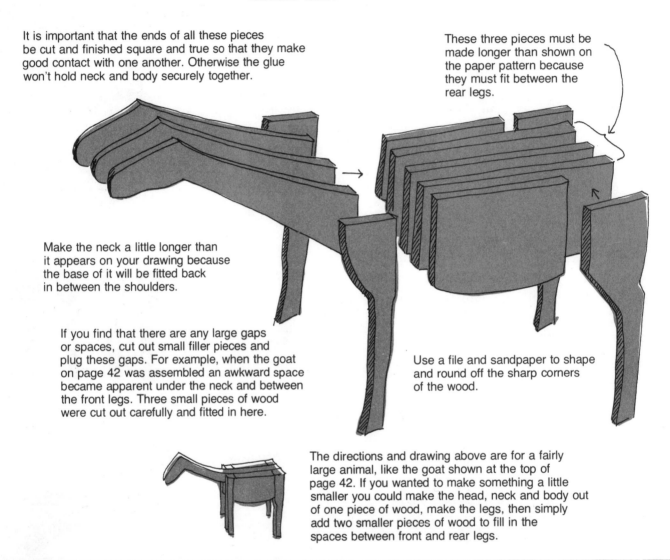

Make the neck a little longer than it appears on your drawing because the base of it will be fitted back in between the shoulders.

If you find that there are any large gaps or spaces, cut out small filler pieces and plug these gaps. For example, when the goat on page 42 was assembled an awkward space became apparent under the neck and between the front legs. Three small pieces of wood were cut out carefully and fitted in here.

Use a file and sandpaper to shape and round off the sharp corners of the wood.

The directions and drawing above are for a fairly large animal, like the goat shown at the top of page 42. If you wanted to make something a little smaller you could make the head, neck and body out of one piece of wood, make the legs, then simply add two smaller pieces of wood to fill in the spaces between front and rear legs.

**10.** By now your goat should begin to look something like a goat, and you can begin to carve some of the more delicate shapes. Take your time, cutting off just a little bit with each stroke of the chisel. Get the sagging back, the big belly, the sharp ridges of hips and shoulders, but don't piddle about with little details. Keep the main forms simple and uncomplicated.

**11.** The horns are sawn or whittled out of a scrap piece of wood. The bases should be rounded off into a peg-like shape and fitted into holes drilled in the top of the head.

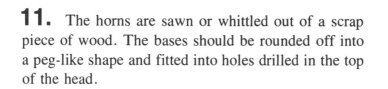

**12.** The tail and beard can be made from a handful of knitting wool, or carved like the horns.

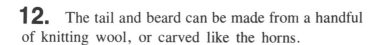

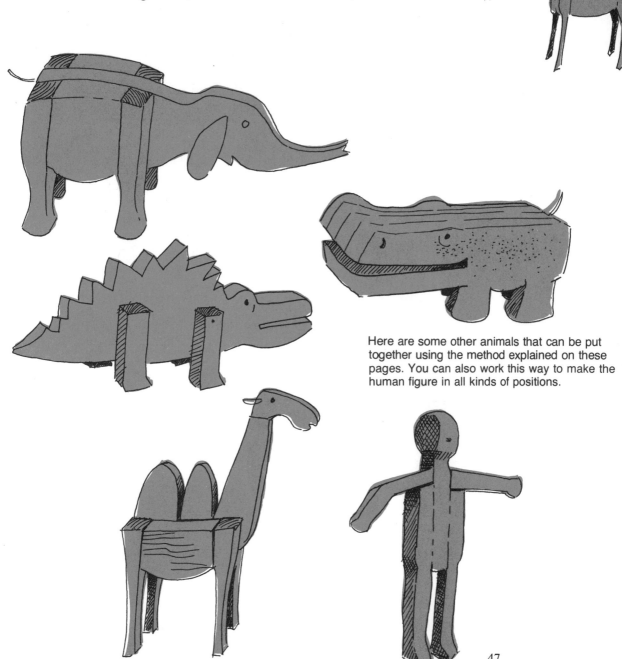

Here are some other animals that can be put together using the method explained on these pages. You can also work this way to make the human figure in all kinds of positions.

47

# MAKING A GOAT

1. A drawing of the goat was first made on a sheet of heavy, brown wrapping paper. The rear leg has been cut out here.

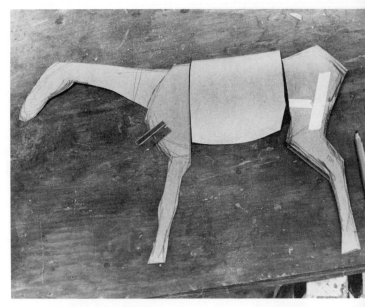

2. All the patterns have been cut out now. There is one for the head and neck, one for the front legs and shoulders, another for the body, and a fourth for the rear legs.

3. The patterns have been traced onto the wood and cut out. Notice how the grain runs.

4. The rest of the wood has been cut out here. The arrangement of all these pieces is shown in the drawing on page 46.

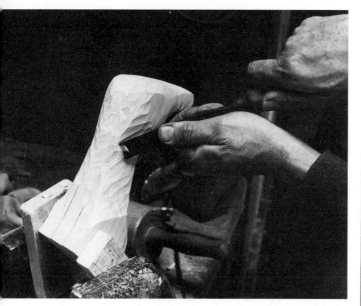

5. The head and neck are the only part that require any really extensive shaping. And this is most conveniently done if these parts are glued together and shaped before attaching to the rest of the goat. A rasp or rough file could do this job as well as a hammer and chisel.

6. All the parts have been glued together. Cracks and gaps have been filled with plastic wood. The stomach and back of the goat have been rounded off and the entire surface smoothed with sandpaper.

7. And here's the finished goat, complete with horns, tail and beard. The eyes have been simply drawn in with a pencil. The color and grain of the wood was so nice, and there was little patching, so no paint was used. A coat of varnish is all that is needed to keep the wood from getting soiled.

8. Here's a close-up view of the head and neck. The mouth is suggested by a thin saw cut and a little filing.

Painted wooden mask from New Guinea,
Chicago Natural History Museum

Painted Northwest Indian mask,
American Museum of Natural History

Mask, American Museum of Natural History.
This was made by Tlingit Indians who live
in the southeast part of Alaska.

Mask from New Caledonia,
Brooklyn Museum

# 8. Wooden Masks and Totem Poles

The kinds of masks shown here were used by many primitive civilizations. Sometimes the masks were used in religious ceremonies or dramatic spectacles. Some Eskimo masks represented magic spirits seen by medicine men. Some represented various gods or were meant to cause rain or insure good hunting. Whatever their original purpose the masks appear to us today as imaginative, colorful objects and often designs of great beauty.

If you decide that you want to carve a mask try making up a few sketches before you start. And by all means don't try to be realistic—the more wild and fanciful the design the better. If you don't feel like making any preliminary drawings just grab your hammer and chisel and start in, even if you haven't the slightest idea of how your mask is going to turn out. Ideas will come to you as you work.

**Materials**      A log that has been split in half is the ideal material for carving a mask. The back of the log can be hollowed out, holes drilled for your eyes, and the mask can be actually held up in front of your face while you do a fierce war dance.

If you can't find a suitable log you can build up a block of wood using two or more short planks of wood glued together. Don't be concerned if this seems like rather flat proportions for a mask. A built up, rounded form can be made by adding pieces of wood for nose or chin or forehead.

There are no step-by-step instructions for making a mask because no two masks will be alike. The kind you make will

Totem pole by **Northwest** Coast Indians, American Museum of Natural History

51

depend on the materials you have and your own ideas about how a mask should look. However, all the wood carving techniques we have discussed in this book are still important. You must keep your chisels sharp, watch the grain of the wood, use separate, attached pieces of wood for any long or thin projections. If there are any defects in your wood, such as knotholes or branches, try to make use of them. See if you can't fit them into the design of your mask.

A good size for a mask is about 8″ wide and 12″ tall, and perhaps 6″ deep. But there is no reason to stick to these dimensions. You could work larger or smaller.

Painted wooden mask from Southern Nigeria, American Museum of Natural History. In the case of this mask, the painting and decorating are just about as important as the carving.

**Painting and Decorating**     If you are pleased with the way your mask looks when you are through carving it there is no reason you can't let it go at that. Simply rub a little wax on it. But most masks are treated a little more elaborately with paint and various applied decorations. If you do decide to paint your mask limit yourself to two or three colors, or two or three groups of closely related colors. Otherwise there is a danger of getting an unpleasant garish look. Actually it is quite effective if you use paint in some areas and leave the natural wood showing in others.

Almost anything can be used for decoration if you think this is called for. You can use nails, tacks, feathers, beads, bones, dried grass, hair, scraps of fur, wool, tin, and just about anything else you can think of.

Part of a totem pole from British Columbia,
American Museum of Natural History

Totem pole by Northwest
Coast Indians, American
Museum of Natural History

## Totem Poles

Totem poles were carved by the Indians of the Northwest. They were supposed to guard against evil spirits and to commemorate various important happenings in the tribe. These totem poles, which were carved out of full grown tree trunks, are often twenty or thirty feet tall and brightly painted. They are very impressive objects.

You can make your own—somewhat smaller—totem pole out of a log or a piece of 4″ by 4″ lumber. It is carved just about the same way as the masks already described, and in fact you might consider a totem pole as a little like a few masks piled one on top of another. (Though totem poles often include animal and human figures as well as heads). One difference, however, is that a totem pole is meant to be viewed from all sides, not just from in front as is the case with a mask.

A totem pole can be made much more lively looking if separate elements are added to form wings, horns, noses, beaks, and so on. If the bases of these additions are whittled into a peg-like shape they can be easily set into appropriate holes drilled or carved into the pole. A little glue will hold them permanently in place. If there are little gaps or spaces these can be filled with plastic wood, putty, or a mixture of glue and sawdust.

If your totem pole is to stand by itself (it could also be hung on a wall) it should have some kind of a base to steady it. A square, neatly sanded piece of board nailed or screwed to the bottom of the pole will do the trick.

53

# MAKING A TOTEM POLE

1. Here is the log we started with. It is 32″ tall and approximately 5″ in diameter. The bark has been stripped off the upper part of the log, but some remains at the bottom.

2. The design has been very roughly sketched on the log and the first carving is started. Because the outer layer of this particular piece of wood is rather dark the chisel marks show up clearly.

3. The basic shapes can be seen now. That blunt nose on the second face from the bottom is made by a lump that projected out from the log. This totem pole has no animal or human figures—only heads.

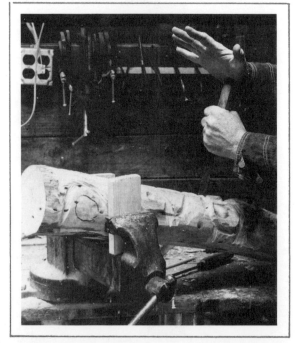

4. Here you can see how the log is supported as it is worked on. One end is held in a vise. The other end rests on the work bench. It is important that it doesn't roll or slip about while being worked on.

5. Assorted ears, wings, and noses have been attached now. This sort of addition will make a totem pole much more lively and interesting.

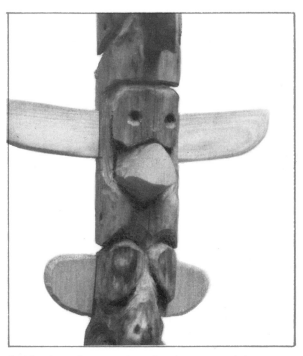

6. Here's a close-up view showing some of the parts that have been added on.

7. This is the finished totem pole. The colors used to paint it were black. white, red, yellow, and blue.

These house numbers
are attached to a
fence.

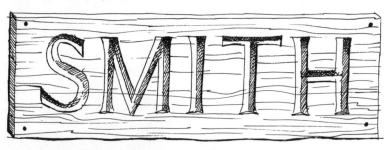

ABEJK
NSW

# 9. Names and Numbers

There are many places where names and numbers will be useful and attractive when carved in wood. If you live in a house in the country or the suburbs the family name or street number is essential for visitors, mailmen, and delivery men. In city apartments the name or apartment number can be attached to the front door, or alongside it and is equally essential.

And there are other uses. You might want a sign saying "private" or a plaque with your name on the door of your room. You might want to have a motto on your wall. A sign of this sort can be a very elegant thing when the lettering is neatly and carefully done.

**Materials**      A flat board is all you need. It should be dry and free of knotholes, not warped or split and of a size to suit your purpose. If the sign is going to go alongside a driveway and must be seen from a distance it should be fairly large size. If you are making a sign for an apartment door you would want it rather small.

**How To Do It**      The secret of carving a good sign is to very carefully lay out the letters or numbers before you start to carve. Unless you are pretty confident in your own lettering skill (you probably aren't because practically nobody knows how to letter well) you can use the letters opposite and below as a guide. Or you can trace them if you are working small. Some of the letters of the alphabet are omitted because you can figure them out from the ones shown. For example, an "F" is the same as an "E" with the lower stroke eliminated.

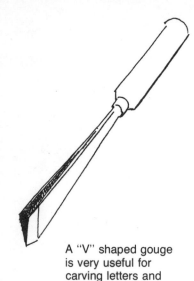

A "V" shaped gouge is very useful for carving letters and numbers.

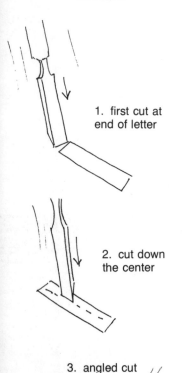

1. first cut at end of letter

2. cut down the center

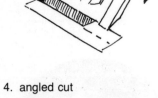

3. angled cut

chip pops out

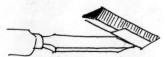

4. angled cut

This is the way to transfer the letters to your wood: **1.** Put a piece of tracing paper over the book and trace the outline of the letters you need. Rule a straight line on your paper to keep the letters straight. **2.** Then put a piece of carbon paper over your wood. Place your tracing paper on top of this. **3.** With a pencil go over the letters, pressing down hard. This will transfer the letters on the tracing paper onto the wood. Now you are ready to go.

Before you actually start work on your sign do some experimenting on scrap wood. It will take a little practice before you learn to get crisp, neat looking letters.

The simplest way to carve letters and numbers in wood is with a V cut. This can be done with a "V" shaped gouge. You simply tap the gouge along, following your traced letters. But this tool isn't always available, and in this case you will have to use a straight-edge chisel. This is how it is done: **1.** Start by making a vertical cut at the end of the letter. If the wood is not terribly hard you can use a pocketknife for this cut, or you can use the straight-edge chisel. **2.** Next a vertical cut is made along the center of the letter. **3.** Another cut is made at an angle along one side of the letter. **4.** Then make another cut from the other side of the letter. This should remove the wood from the center.

This works fine for straight letters. But what happens when you come to the curved part of the letter "D" for example? In this case you will have to slowly cut at an angle, carefully following the curve. Make one cut along the outside of the curve, another along the inside. When you do this you must pay great attention to the way the grain is running. You never want to cut into or against the grain. This will cause splits and splinters. It is also very important that your tools be extremely sharp for this kind of cutting.

When you have all the letters carved you may decide to use paint to increase their legibility. This is important if the sign is to be seen from a distance. Paint the letters, and don't worry if the paint goes over the edges. When the paint is dried you can sand the surface of the wood thoroughly, this will remove any paint that has gotten out of the grooves. Finally varnish or shellac the wood. This is especially important if it is going to be out in the weather.

1. These photographs show the steps in carving a name plate for the stern of a boat. The first step is to draw the letters on paper, working as neatly and carefully as possible. The final carving can't be any better looking than the original drawing.

2. The letters have been traced onto the wood and the carving started. Notice the vertical cut that runs along the center bar of the letter "N." The tool shown in the photograph is a small "V" shaped gouge which is useful for fine lines and curves.

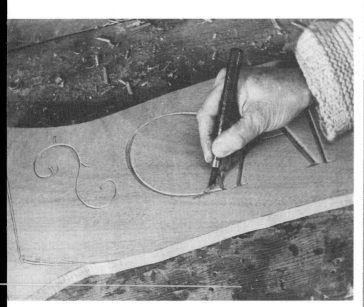

3. The letters have all been carved now and a small, sharp knife is being used to make corrections and to widen some of the strokes. Here, as in all carving, it is important to pay attention to the direction of the grain.

4. The name plate is almost finished now. All that remains to be done is apply a coat of varnish to protect the wood from the weather.

THE KISS, Constantin Brancusi, limestone,
Philadelphia Museum of Art

# Part Two
# CARVING STONE

## 1. Tools and Materials

Most people who have never tried to carve stone have the idea that it is a terribly difficult kind of work that requires enormous experience and great strength and skill. This might be true if you were going to attempt something like Michelangelo's *David,* which is larger than life size and cut out of a block of marble weighing many tons. But the simpler, more compact kind of carving like the one illustrated on the opposite page, is no more difficult to carve out of stone than they would be out of wood. In fact in some ways stone is easier than wood to work with. There is very little problem of grain. A chisel can be directed in any direction in stone without fear of causing splitting or splintering.

Stone is, of course, a hard material. It is one of the most durable materials and has been used by sculptors as far back as history records. But, like wood, there are many different kinds. Some of them are actually softer than wood. Alabaster, which is a frequently used stone, can be cut with a pocketknife. Ebony, on the other hand, is a tough wood that requires hammer and chisel to carve.

If you are going to try carving stone you need a *suitable* piece of stone, and the proper tools.

## Kinds of Stone

The kinds of stone that are best for a beginner are a not too hard marble or a piece of limestone. Vermont marble, Tennessee marble, Georgia marble, and Alabama marble are all suitable for carving. (As you can see, marble is often named after the place it comes from.) Most any kind of limestone is good. Alabaster and soapstone are relatively soft and easy to carve. There are many different Italian marbles which have been used for sculpture for thousands of years. Michelangelo used to make trips to the quarries of Carrara, a town on the western side of Italy. He would actually choose from the mountainside the particular piece of stone he wanted to carve. The quarry men would then cut it out of the mountain, square it off, and truck it to the sculptor's studio. But it is not very likely that you will be able to obtain your stone in this way!

## Where To Get It

It is not always easy to find stone that can be easily carved. There is always a lot of stone lying around on the ground. Rocks and boulders are everywhere. But, unfortunately, most of this kind of stone isn't any good for carving. A lot of it will be granite, which is an extremely hard stone, much too difficult for the amateur. A lot of the other field stones you'll find are a mixture of several different kinds of stone. And this is no good either. If you see some stone that seems promising try chipping away at it and see what happens. If you find that you can easily "shave" off an even, thin layer of the stone it means you have a good piece that can be used. If your chisel just bounces off without cutting into the stone, it is too hard or brittle and of no use.

In many parts of the country there are old quarries where you can find odd, left-over chunks of stone. The states that are located along the Appalachian mountains, which run north and south along the eastern part of the United States, have many marble deposits and there are many quarries. Actually, there are quarries just about everywhere. Some produce granite or hard marbles which you don't want; others will have stone that is easily carved. If you know of an abandoned quarry you should be able to find plenty of good-sized pieces of stone lying

HEAD OF CHRIST, William Zorach, black granite, The Museum of Modern Art, New York. Granite is one of the most difficult materials to carve. It is extremely dense and compact.

MAIZE GOD, Honduras, limestone, American Museum of Natural History. Limestone is a very rugged material, but not too hard for a beginner at stone carving.

around which may be free for the taking. If you know of a working quarry you will have to ask for permission to take any odd pieces you fancy.

Another possible source of stone or marble is the site where a building is being torn down. You won't find anything if it is a simple wood structure that is being razed. But if the building was large and well built you may be lucky and come across some fancy marble from old fireplaces or bannisters or some good stone from the foundation.

Sometimes old cemeteries have a rubble heap off in a back corner. Old, replaced pieces of tombstones or bases of tombstones that have been discarded are dumped here. Poke around and see if you can find something useful. Here again, be sure to avoid the very hard granite. (Granite is usually gray or pink and has a kind of mottled salt and pepper pattern.)

Another possible source is a large art store or sculpture supply store. Here you can buy small blocks of alabaster or soapstone, both of which are easy to carve and good for the beginning carver.

Getting a good piece of stone to carve can be a bit of a problem. But with perserverence, a good deal of poking around, and some luck, you will eventually find something suitable.

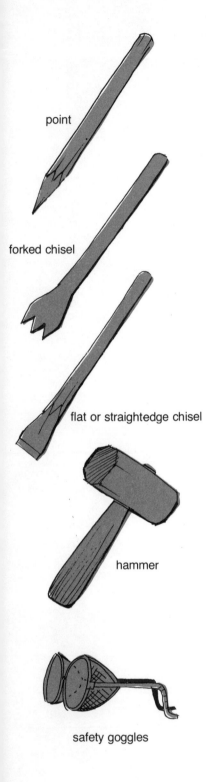

point

forked chisel

flat or straightedge chisel

hammer

safety goggles

## The Tools

There are four basic tools for carving stone.

**1. The Point**     As the name implies this is simply a chisel that comes to a point. It is used for the first roughing-out operation.

**2. The Toothed Chisel**     This tool is like a flat chisel, except that it has teeth. It is a little like a stubby fork, and it is used after the main forms have been carved with the point.

**3. The Flat Chisel**     This is the finishing tool. You can get flat surfaces and fine detail with this chisel.

**4. The Hammer**     It is possible to use an ordinary carpenter's claw hammer, or a ball peen hammer, if you have nothing else. But there are special stone cutting hammers. They are stubby and quite heavy, and they make carving a lot smoother and easier. A lightweight hammer is no help at all. It will bounce off the head of the chisel without conveying any weight or power to the stone.

**Safety Goggles**     These are not really a tool, but they are *absolutely essential*. Chips fly up with enormous speed and they can very easily hit you in the eye. So don't ever attempt to carve stone unless you are wearing them!

The chisels listed above come in a variety of sizes. Flat chisels, for example, are available one-fourth inch wide up to more than one inch wide. Toothed chisels can have three, six or more teeth, and the points also come in different thicknesses. If you have only one of each of these tools a good selection would be a 3/8″ point (this refers to the diameter of the steel rod from which the point is made), a 5/8″ flat chisel, and a three-tooth chisel. These tools can be sharpened on a grindstone or on a flat, coarse carborundum sharpening stone.

These tools are available from any sculpture supply store or a large art store. If the art store doesn't stock these tools they usually can order them for you. There are not many blacksmith shops left in this country, but if you happen to know of one the tools can be easily made there.

It is also possible to use a variety of make-shift tools if the stone you are using isn't too hard. Hardware stores have what are called "cold chisels." These are intended for cutting metal. But they can be used for cutting stone if you can't get the proper stone cutting chisels. You might also make use of a "punch." This is short and you couldn't give it a really good wallop without danger to your thumb, but it is better than nothing. If your stone is alabaster or soapstone you can use heavyweight, carpenter's wood cutting chisels. But once you use them on stone they won't be much good for wood anymore. You might also try sharpening some large, old screwdrivers to get a narrow flat chisel.

Most stone can be brought to a smooth, polished surface. And to do this you need files or rasps, abrasive stones, and sandpaper. The smoothing is done just as you would do it with a piece of wood, gradually using finer and finer abrasives until you get the finish you want. The color and beauty of a nice piece of stone doesn't really become apparent until it is given a fine polish.

## Using the Tools

Stone cutting tools are used to "shave" the stone—never crush or maul it. The tools are held at about a forty-five degree angle to the work. The tool is never pointed directly into the stone because this will ruin the tool and possibly cause the stone to split in two. As you work on stone you will get a feeling about how the tools should be held and used. Don't try to carve with dull, blunted tools.

Stone, like wood, or any material is strong in some ways, weak in others. Stone is enormously strong when it is in a compact, block-like shape. It can't be very easily compressed or crushed. This is one of the reasons it is used so much as a building material. On the other hand, a piece of stone that is long or thin will easily break.

For this reason it is best to avoid thin, delicate shapes. Sharp noses, delicate ears, outstretched arms, and shapes of this sort are best avoided. These shapes are not only liable to break off, but are extremely difficult to carve. Remember that all carving is a "subtractive" process. If you want a shape to stick out you must remove all the material surrounding that shape.

If you look at the stone carvings reproduced in this book

you'll see very few thin, pointy forms. Most of the forms are compact, bunched up.

The usual way of working when you carve is to do all the preliminary work with the pointed chisel, or "point" as it is called. A great deal of the roughing out can be done with this tool. The forked chisel is used next, and then the finishing off and detail work is done with the straightedge chisel. The final step is the polishing.

# 2. Making a Stone Carving

In any carving—particularly stone carving—what you decide to carve is often determined by the original shape of the stone. If, for example, you happened to find a stubby, round piece of stone, the sculpture you would make would most likely be stubby and rounded. If the stone was tall and narrow the sculpture would be tall and narrow. The reason for this is that it is simply too much work and too tedious to cut away large amounts of unwanted material. It is much easier to choose a design that will fit into the shape of the stone.

Sometimes a sculptor will have a very definite idea about what he wants to make. Then he will set out to look for a stone that is suitable. But most amateurs can't just order the size and shape of stone they want. They will have to settle for what they can get and then think of a subject to fit.

Many professional stone carvers will have pieces of stone lying around their studios for a long time—sometimes many years. When they get an idea that fits in with a particular piece of stone they will begin to carve it, not before.

There is an infinite variety of sizes and shapes of stone to be found, and there is no telling what kind you will be able to get. So, for this reason, there is no point in giving any specific suggestions here as to what you should carve. What you do will be determined by the stone you have as well as your own ideas and preferences.

In this section there are a number of illustrations of carvings which will give you some idea of the sort of thing that can be done. And on the next few pages are a very detailed explanation and demonstration of how a turtle was carved out of a block of limestone. If you read this carefully you will have a good idea of how the tools are handled and how the shapes and forms evolve.

I made the carving described here in order to show the way one particular sculptor (me) worked and how the various tools were used. If this were your piece of stone you would no doubt have altogether different ideas about what to do and how to proceed. But at any rate this will introduce you to some of the problems and some of the thinking involved in carving a piece of stone.

## CARVING A TURTLE

1. This is the block of stone I started with. I found it half covered with dirt and weeds in a back corner of my garden. Because it had been squared off I suspect that it had been used at one time as part of a foundation for a building or as a boundary marker. When I first came upon it I thought it might be a piece of concrete. But it had a brownish color and it wasn't sandy in texture. So I decided it was limestone. I made an experimental cut with a straight-edge chisel and the stone cut fairly smoothly and evenly, which further convinced me it wasn't concrete.

2. Here are the tools I used: Point, forked chisel, straightedge chisel, hammer, and safety goggles.

3. Stone carving is a messy business, so I worked out of doors, using a piece of log as a work bench. Here the point is being used to round off the top of the stone.

4. The top has been roughed out and the forked chisel has been used to cut the half circle in which the turtle's head will be placed.

5. The space around the turtle's head has been cut out and the basic, rough shape of eyes and nose have been developed.

6. At this point I decided that the feet of the turtle should be shown. So the base of the stone was cut back leaving the stone out of which the feet could be carved.

7. The shell has been shaped a little more carefully now. The edge of the shell has been carved in a graceful, curved line. A straightedge chisel, then a file has been used on the front edge of the shell.

8. Here's a back view of the turtle. The shell has been gone over thoroughly with a file to remove all the chisel marks and get as smooth and rounded a surface as possible. The marks of the toothed chisel have been left on the base however.

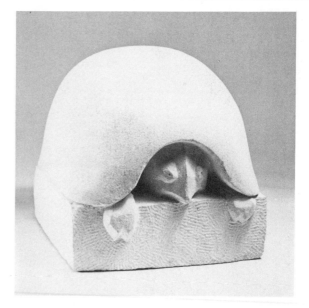

9. Here's the finished piece. He sits on the front steps of my house now, greeting all visitors and guests, and I give him a friendly pat every time I come and go.

STONE HEAD, Mexico,
American Museum of Natural History

STONE FIGURE, Mexico, American Museum of
Natural History. The very compact forms
of this sculpture, with no deep cutting,
suggest the hardness of the stone.

CAPITAL, Isamu Noguchi, Georgia Marble, The Museum of
Modern Art, New York. This carving, which fits on top
of a pole is completely abstract. The curves and shapes and
smooth white texture of the stone were all that the
sculptor was interested in.

HEAD, Easter Islands, American Museum of Natural
History. Heads like these were carved out of volcanic
stone by a race of people we know very little about. The
stones weigh many tons and some of them stand twenty
or more feet tall.

70

HEAD, Amedeo Modigliani, limestone, The Museum of Modern Art, New York. This was carved in 1915 in Paris by a sculptor who had seen and been influenced by wooden African mask carvings. The narrow dimensions of the piece of stone he had to work with determined to some extent the shape of the carving.

LION, The Metropolitan Museum of Art. This is a 14th century Italian carving.

FISH, Constantin Brancusi, The Museum of Modern Art, New York. Even though this is the most simple, flat form with absolutely no details, the graceful curves give the feeling of a fish in water. The marble has been highly polished and mounted with great care on a base that shows it off to best advantage.

71

HAWK-GOD HORUS, The Metropolitan Museum of Art. This Egyptian sculpture was carved out of basalt, which is an extremely hard stone.

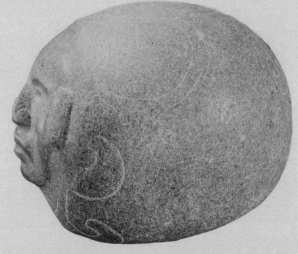

HEAD, Mexico, American Museum of Natural History. This sculpture looks very much like a boulder one might find lying about in a field. Judging by the simple surface decoration and minimal carving, it is a hard stone, probably granite.

HEAD, Chaim Gross, Alabaster. This is an easy to carve stone that has a lovely color and translucency.

736    Weiss, Harvey
WEI
       Carving: how to
       carve wood and
       stone

| DATE | | | |
|---|---|---|---|
| MAY 1 | | | |
| APR 4 | | | |
| | | | |
| AR 27 | | | |
| | | | |
| | | | |
| | | | |
| | | | |
| | | | |
| | | | |
| | | | |
| | | | |